SHEFFIELD
ROUND
WALK

A 24km/15mile scenic city walk
through parks and woodland

Vertebrate Publishing, Sheffield
www.**v-publishing**.co.uk

SHEFFIELD ROUND WALK

A 24km/15mile scenic city walk
through parks and woodland

Jon Barton

SHEFFIELD ROUND WALK

Jon Barton

First published in 2020 by Vertebrate Publishing. Reprinted in 2021.

 Vertebrate Publishing
Omega Court, 352 Cemetery Road, Sheffield S11 8FT, United Kingdom.
www.v-publishing.co.uk

Copyright © 2020 Jon Barton and Vertebrate Publishing Ltd.

Jon Barton has asserted his rights under the Copyright, Designs and Patents Act 1988 to be identified as author of this work.

A CIP catalogue record for this book is available from the British Library.

ISBN 978-1-912560-83-7

Front cover: Forge Dam.
All photography by Adam Long unless otherwise credited.

 All maps reproduced by permission of Ordnance Survey
on behalf of The Controller of Her Majesty's Stationery Office.
© Crown Copyright. 100025218.

Design by Jane Beagley, production by Cameron Bonser – www.v-publishing.co.uk

Printed and bound in Europe by Pulsio.

Vertebrate Publishing is committed to printing on paper from sustainable sources.

Contents

Introduction . . . . **vii**

Acknowledgements . . . . **viii**

Run or walk? . . . . **viii**

Walk times . . . . **x**

The Countryside Code . . . . **x**

Maps, descriptions, distances . . . . **x**

Km/mile conversion chart . . . . **xi**

Sheffield Area Map . . . . **xii**

1 Porter Valley **1**

2 Limb Valley **15**

3 Sheaf Valley **27**

4 Gleadless Valley **37**

Further information **48**

Meersbrook Park

Introduction

The Sheffield Round Walk is one of the most scenic, long urban walks in the UK. Because of the wide variety of habitats encountered on the Round Walk the flora and fauna is justifiably varied. Predominantly parkland, from wild and ancient woodlands through to manicured playing fields, the walk also covers gardens, urban development, rivers, streams, ponds, lakes, farmland, allotments, golf courses, meadows and hedgerows.

The path uses well-marked good trails and short sections of roadside footpath to link each section. The walk is well signposted by distinctive green signposts and acorn waymarkers. A fine tradition is to look out for all three species of British woodpecker – the great spotted, the lesser spotted and the green – all big fans of the walk. The woodland is a mix of ancient and some plantation, much continuously wooded since at least the sixteenth century. Mature oak and beech woodlands fill the lower valley sides, with birch and rowan common in the higher cloughs, alder in wetter areas and ash on the field margins.

Jon Barton

Acknowledgements

This book would not have been possible without the help of Adam Long, who contributed his expert knowledge on the nature and landscape of the Sheffield Round Walk, and Martin Whiteley, for input on the geology that shapes the walk. Also thanks to my family, Gràinne and Thomas, who have often walked sections of the walk with me, and my running buddy, Bret, who has paced me through Graves Park on more than one occasion. Thanks to Sheffield City Council and the Outdoor City team for help and encouragement, and lastly and most importantly the team at Vertebrate – my editor Helen Parry, John Coefield, Lorna Hargreaves and Cameron Bonser – who have seen this book through to publication and sold it to you.

Run or walk?

The Round Walk is quite a length and doesn't have any obvious shortcuts, except perhaps the Porter Valley and the Limb Valley. This Porter and Limb section could be missed out or done as a separate circuit in its own right, especially with the cheeky use of a bus to complete the Ecclesall Road link. The terrain on the Round Walk is never tough; most of the walk is on hard-packed, all-weather paths, many tarmac, although never so much as to detract from the experience. Good walking shoes or light boots rather than heavy boots would be ideal footwear. As for the runner, there is an annual staged race which follows this route: the Round Sheffield Run. Running the complete route is a rite of passage for any local distance runner. The terrain is varied, much hill climbing to test the power, plenty of pacy trails to keep the time keen and little navigation to cause a distraction. A trail shoe is fine, don't rush the road crossings. The walker will want to take all day, and certainly plan to have lunch in the Norfolk Arms at Ringinglow or the Rose Garden Cafe in Graves Park depending on an early or late start. For the runner – well it's perfect for a summer evening after work isn't it? A good two hours, or more like three. You'll be chasing the bats along Brincliffe Edge, but what a way to finish a working day.

The walk can be started anywhere but is described from Endcliffe Park, through the Porter Valley to Ringinglow, descending through the Limb Valley and Ecclesall Woods, before climbing through Ladies' Spring Wood, Chancet Wood and across Graves Park. A finale through the Gleadless Valley, Meersbrook Park, Brincliffe Edge Wood and Chelsea Park concludes this 15-mile walk.

Near the top of the Porter Valley
Photo: Dom Worrall,
Round Sheffield Run

Walk times

The walk is approximately 24km/15miles long and takes six to seven hours to complete. It is split into four sections of roughly equal length. Walk times should allow you to complete the walk at a pace that's comfortable for most regular walkers, allowing you time to enjoy the views and an occasional photo stop. Allow extra time to stop for refreshments at one of the excellent cafes or pubs along the route.

The Countryside Code

Respect Protect Enjoy

Respect **other people**
· Consider the local community and other people enjoying the outdoors
· Leave gates and property as you find them and follow paths unless wider access is available

Protect **the natural environment**
· Leave no trace of your visit and take your litter home
· Keep dogs under effective control

Enjoy **the outdoors**
· Plan ahead and be prepared
· Follow advice and local signs

Maps, descriptions, distances

While every effort has been made to maintain accuracy within the maps and descriptions in this guide, we are unable to guarantee that every single detail is correct. Please exercise caution if a direction or a sign appears at odds with the route on the map. If in doubt, a comparison of the route description with the maps in this book (along with a bit of common sense) should help ensure that you're on the right track. The Ordnance Survey (OS) map that covers this walk is OS 1:25,000 Explorer 278 Sheffield & Barnsley.

Please treat stated distances as a guideline only. OS maps, which are included with the route descriptions in this book, are commonly used, are easy to read and many people are happy using them. If you're not familiar with OS maps and are unsure of what the symbols mean, you can download a free OS 1:25,000 map legend from **www.ordnancesurvey.co.uk**

Km/mile conversion chart

Metric to Imperial
1 kilometre [km] » 1,000 m » 0.6214 mile
1 metre [m] » 100 cm » 1.0936 yd
1 centimetre [cm] » 10 mm » 0.3937 in
1 millimetre [mm] » 0.03937 in

Imperial to Metric
1 mile » 1,760 yd » 1.6093 km
1 yard [yd] » 3 ft » 0.9144 m
1 foot [ft] » 12 in » 0.3048 m
1 inch [in] » 2.54 cm

Looking down the Porter Valley
towards Sheffield

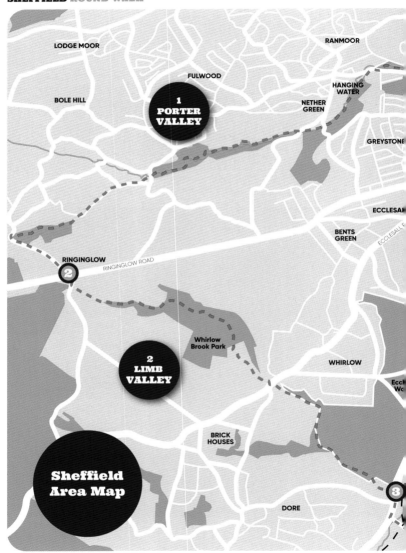

FE
NT

ffe
k

S

ECCLESALL ROAD

**SHARROW
VALE**

**LITTLE
SHEFFIELD**

HIGHFIELD

**SHARROW
HEAD**

SHARROW

LOWFIELD

BRINCLIFFE

HEELEY

Chelsea
Park

**NETHER
EDGE**

**CARTER
KNOWLE**

**MEERSBROOK
BANK**

MEERSBROOK

**Gleadless
Valley
Woodland
Park**

**NORTON
LEES**

**FOURLANE
ENDS**

1ILLHOUSES

ABBEYDALE ROAD

CHESTERFIELD ROAD

**NORTON
WOODSEATS**

**4
GLEADLESS
VALLEY**

4

BACKMOOR

Animal
Farm

Graves Park

**MEADOW
HEAD**

NORTON

**3
SHEAF
VALLEY**

BEAUCHIEF

GREENHILL

Mill race near Forge Dam

1

PORTER VALLEY

Hunter's Bar Roundabout
Endcliffe Park
Bingham Park
Shepherd Wheel
Whiteley Woods
Forge Dam
Porter Clough
Mayfield Alpacas
Ringinglow

Finish

The Norfolk Arms,
Ringinglow Road, S11 7TS
Grid reference
SK 291837

Start

Hunter's Bar Roundabout,
Ecclesall Road, S11 8TF
Grid reference
SK 332857

Distance

5.6km/3.5miles

Terrain

Public footpaths,
bridleways and roads,
can be muddy in
parts during winter

Fulwood

Goo
Gree

Hill

Bole Hill
Farm

Bennet
Grange

289

Fulwood
Hall

259

David Lane
Farm

254 Mill Lane
Farm

Douse Croft
Farm

287

FB

Mill
House

196

Weirs

Priest Hill
Low Farm

Whiteley W

Old May
House

Foxhall Lane

FB

House

Bassett
Houses

Bassett
Cottages

Green House
Farm

Clough Lane

Priest
Hill

234

College Lane

Hangram Lane
Farm

341

Porter
Clough

Clough Hollow

Moorfield
Farm

Brown Edge

FARM
ATTRACTION

Ringinglow

306

Resr

Wigley
Farm

Firs
Farm

ARCHERY

331

6

358

w Road

Moor
Cott

332

Smeltings
Farm

321

Bole Hill
Plantation

FBs

Limb Val

Ranmoor

Sch

FBs

Weirs

FBs

FBs

FB

Weirs

FBs

FB

FB

FBs

Hanging
Water

Bingham
Park

Endcliffe
Park

Schs

Sch

Nether
Green

FBs

Sch

FBs

Weir

Allot
Gdns

Greystones
Cliffe

Greystones

Sch

Brincliffe

Porter Valley
Woodlands
Nature Reserve

FB

Sch

Sch

Brincliffe
Tower
168

Banner
Cross

Brincliffe Edge

Ecclesall

Sch

Liby

Carter
Knowle

Hill
Top

PO

Bents
Green

Sch

School

Sch

ryft
ouse

Parkhead

FBs

Schs

Sch

226

3

Previous page: Looking down the Porter Valley towards Sheffield

Top left: The Porter Brook in Whiteley Woods

Top right: Endcliffe Park

Inset: Mandarin ducks

Right: Endcliffe Park

Far right: Heron in Whiteley Woods

Far right bottom: Primroses

The Sheffield Round Walk starts from Hunter's Bar Roundabout on Ecclesall Road (A625). The old toll gate is still in evidence in the middle of the roundabout – it was active until the late nineteenth century, when a rapid need for housing overtook the area. Fortunately Endcliffe Park has remained development free. The park has several monuments dedicated to Queen Victoria, as well as a small plaque on the site of a World War II aircraft crash site – an emotive incident in which a damaged plane, hoping to land on the playing field, crashed into the hillside to avoid children playing in the park. It is through this park that the walk begins. **Start** on the roundabout at the open gateway; keeping the Porter Brook to your right, **follow the tarmac path** up to and past the children's playground then onwards. Traversing this popular park, always following the Porter Brook, keep an eye out for brown trout, herons and kingfishers near the water. On this section of the walk a number of millponds and dams can be seen which once provided the water powering Sheffield's metalworking industries. Leave Endcliffe Park and **cross over** Rustlings Road, **heading into** Bingham Park and Whiteley Woods.

THE
ADJOINING
LAND OF 15
ACRES 1R 19P WAS
BY SUBSCRIPTION AND PRESENTED
TO THE CORPORATION OF SHEFFIELD
FOR THE PURPOSE OF A
PUBLIC RECREATION GROUND
IN COMMEMORATION OF THE JUBILEE OF
HER MAJESTY QUEEN VICTORIA
1887

Top left: Mill race in Whiteley Woods

Top right: Woodland near Forge Dam

Follow the broad tarmac path through the park. The path passes Shepherd Wheel which is worth a quick explore. Shepherd Wheel was a water-powered grinding workshop; it is thought to have been used primarily for the grinding of table and other domestic knives as well as penknives and pocketknives. It derives its name from its connection with a Mr Shepherd who, in 1794, employed ten men there. The restoration of Shepherd Wheel which is listed as a scheduled ancient monument was first conceived in 1926. Over the intervening years negotiations proceeded for its preservation and restoration, culminating in 1954 with the formation of the Council for the Conservation of Sheffield Antiquities who, together with the help of numerous firms and volunteers, carried out a programme of restoration to the buildings. It offers a fascinating insight into Sheffield's past. Despite its tranquil setting in acres of glorious woodland, the interior gives some impression of the horrendous working conditions experienced by the grinders. At dusk bats emerge from the eaves to hunt insects around the pond and nearby woodland glades.

After Shepherd Wheel **cross over** Hangingwater Road, leaving the tarmac paths behind now, and **continue walking** through Whiteley Woods, **crossing** Whiteley Wood Road, then up through thick woodland until you reach tarmac and a lovely mill race. **Turn left then right** to arrive at Forge Dam, with its famous children's slide, cafe and the last of the Porter millponds.

Above left: Shepherd Wheel Dam
Above right: Forge Dam Cafe

Top left: Horses in the Porter Valley

Top right: Forge Dam

Inset: Long-tailed tit

Right and far right: The Porter Valley

If you are keen to see all of the three species of woodpeckers this stretch is a good place to start looking. The great spotted woodpecker is a common, conspicuous and fairly noisy bird, and might be encountered in any of the woods along the walk – listen particularly for the incessant squeaky begging of the chicks in late spring. The lesser spotted woodpecker is far more elusive. Only the size of a sparrow and reclusive in behaviour it is one of the fastest declining species in Europe, Yorkshire being one area which is bucking the trend. It particularly favours river woodlands with alder – like the Porter and Limb valleys – and is best spotted in the treetops in early spring before the leaves appear. The green woodpecker is the biggest of the three but prefers more open habitats where it feeds mainly on ants; listen for its laughing 'que-que-que' call and watch for a yellow rump in undulating flight.

Right: The Porter Brook

Walk past the dam and on through the woodland and then **cross over** Wood Cliffe. The walk now takes on a more Peak District feel; the dog walkers and Sunday strollers thin out, replaced by fell runners and other such wildlife. This is Porter Clough, the headwaters of one of Sheffield's five rivers; the path becomes a little steeper and a bit more muddy before breaking out of its beautiful mature beech and pine woodland on to Fulwood Lane at the parking lay-by at Fulwood Head. **Turn left** along Fulwood Lane towards the village of Ringinglow. Looking uphill you might just catch a glimpse of the Peak District moorland, and in spring listen out for the beautiful bubbling call of the few remaining curlew. This upland fringe is also a well-known corridor for migrant birds that can turn up anything from great grey shrike to osprey, as well being used daily by huge numbers of common birds such as woodpigeon. Look out too for the unique local breed of long-necked sheep on the left before you get to Ringinglow. **Turn left** along Ringinglow Road to arrive at The Norfolk Arms at Ringinglow village.

Eat, drink and explore

Made by Jonty

A quick meander from Hunter's Bar Roundabout you'll find Jonty's – a popular cafe ideal for a coffee before you start the walk or something more substantial at the end. The all-day breakfast is particularly popular.

363 Sharrow Vale Road, S11 8ZG
07803 082 488
www.madebyjonty.co.uk

Woody's Sandwich Bar

If you need a bacon sandwich before you tackle the walk call at Woody's before you set off. Just off Hunter's Bar Roundabout, they sell a massive range of imaginative hot and cold freshly made sandwiches, drinks and cake. There are only a couple of seats indoors, but there are plenty of benches in Endcliffe Park.

645 Ecclesall Road, Sheffield S11 8PT
0114 267 6122

Endcliffe Park Cafe

Lovely, traditional park cafe, selling a wide variety of sandwiches, main meals, cakes, drinks and ice cream. There is plenty of indoor and outdoor seating with lovely views across the park.

Rustlings Road, S11 7AB
0114 266 3044

Shepherd Wheel

See the working water wheel, workshops and dam. Free admission. Open every weekend and on Bank Holiday Mondays throughout the year.

Whiteley Woods, Off Hangingwater Road, S11 2YE
0114 272 2106
www.simt.co.uk

Forge Dam Cafe

A Sheffield institution, this cafe is in a lovely location next to the river just below the millpond. The menu offers a good selection of snacks and meals, with drinks, cakes and ice cream.

Brookhouse Hill, Sheffield, S10 3TE
0114 263 0265
www.forgedamcafe.co.uk

Mayfield Alpacas

See these fascinating animals thriving on the green fields of Ringinglow. There is also a small coffee shop. Small admission charge.

Quicksaw Farm, Fulwood Lane, Ringinglow Village, S10 4LH
0114 263 0033
www.mayfieldanimalpark.co.uk

The Norfolk Arms

This pub at Ringinglow Village on the edge of the moors has lovely views back down the Porter Valley towards Sheffield. It offers a wide variety of traditional pub food as well as vegetarian, vegan and gluten free options.

2 Ringinglow Village, Ringinglow Road, S11 7TS
0114 230 2197
www.norfolkarms.com

2

LIMB VALLEY

Ringinglow Village
Limb Valley
Whirlow Brook Park
Whinfell Quarry Garden
Ecclesall Woods
J.G. Graves Woodland Discovery Centre
Abbeydale Miniature Railway

Finish

Abbeydale Road South,
S17 3LB
Grid reference
SK 323815

Start

The Norfolk Arms,
Ringinglow Road, S11 7TS
Grid reference
SK 291837

Distance

5.6km/3.5miles

Terrain

Public footpaths
and bridleways, can
be muddy in parts
during winter

Top left and top right: The Limb Valley above Whirlow Brook Park

Right: The Limb Brook near Whirlow Brook Park

From The Norfolk Arms, **cross over** Ringinglow Road and walk **straight ahead** along Sheephill Road, passing the Roundhouse (a former toll house where the octagonal shape allowed the toll-keeper to spot road users from all directions to collect their tolls).

Proceed along Sheephill Road for 100 metres and then **take the footpath on the left** in the dip. This leads down across a field following the Limb Brook. This is the furthest point on the walk from the city centre. **Head down the Limb Valley**. The derelict barn on the right just before the first gate is all that remains of a nineteenth-century smelting operation, using local coal and ore dug from the surrounding fields. Open fields give way to thick lush woodland; lower down there are some of the finest beech trees in Sheffield. A pleasant meandering path, it crosses the brook in a couple of places before hugging the valley side. All too soon the path once again reaches the valley bottom, just before the first silted-up dam. On the right is Whirlow Brook Park; to reach it **turn right and cross over the sturdy stone bridge** (not any of the plethora of boardwalk

bridges) to walk up the path through pine trees. However, one can carry straight on here down the main Limb Brook track – it is no quicker but does miss out Whirlow Brook Park. Enter the magnificent grounds of Whirlow Brook Hall with for once entirely ornamental ponds and a fine collection of trees. Whirlow Brook Hall is often used for weddings, but the grounds are open to the public.

On the ponds in this area look out for the flamboyant little mandarin duck, an oriental species now well established in the quieter woodlands hereabouts. In winter you might also see the occasional goosander, a large if slim duck with wary habits and a long narrow bill used for catching fish. Once through the grounds **follow the driveway downhill**, a short deviation footpath on the left soon links back up with the driveway. Emerge on Ecclesall Road South (A625) by Whinfell Quarry Garden.

Whinfell Quarry Garden was created in 1898 by the Sheffield steel magnate Samuel Doncaster. He had collected thousands of plant specimens from his travels

around the world and created the gardens to house these rare species, cleverly making use of the shelter the quarry provided to create a unique microclimate suited to his exotic finds.

You will find Scots pine, redwood, spruce, birch, elm and beech, western hemlock, cedar and Japanese maple if you take the time to detour through the quarry. Planned for the perennial visitor, there is something of interest in flower, fruit, berry and foliage throughout the year; May is particularly spectacular when the many mature rhododendron are in full bloom.

I guess now is as good a time as any to talk about geology. We are walking here on the eastern side of the great Pennine anticline – a dome-like fold running north to south that forms the spine of northern England – and the slopes reflect the eastward dip of the strata. In the river valleys the rocks themselves can be seen: sandstone beds often protrude, occasionally forming little waterfalls in riverbeds, and coal beds are close to the surface in a number of places including at

the head of the Limb Valley; look at the banks of the
brook as you start the descent of the valley. Coal also
breaks through in Ecclesall Woods and on the banks
of the River Sheaf, although never really in economic
quantities, so there is no danger of stumbling down an
old mine. These 'coal measures', as they are called, are
the result of great river and delta systems from the late
Carboniferous period, a time when the land was thickly
forested and high oxygen levels allowed the evolution
of giant insects and amphibians. The coal deposits –
extensive worldwide – formed from dead wood in the
eons between the first appearance of trees and the
evolution of fungi capable of breaking down lignin.
Outcrops at the top of Ladies' Spring and Brincliffe
are known as 'greenmoor rock', once a huge channel
river and delta flowing into an ancient lake. Finally, the
rather old 'rough rock' makes the surface, marking the
boundary between rural and the moorland landscape
of the Peak District. Look out for old buildings with
stone-flagged roofs in Sheffield; these are often the
much-prized rough rock sandstone.

Top left: Whinfell Quarry Garden

Top right: The Limb Valley
Photo: Round Sheffield Run

Left: Rock formations in the
Limb Valley

Cross Ecclesall Road South and take the path on to a small dirt track on the opposite side of the road. This takes you into a big green field with the woods and Limb Brook on your left. Walk down the left-hand side of Whirlow Playing Fields – just a massive green field with perhaps a solitary dog walker. Head straight down to a **stile gap in the wall** and into Ecclesall Woods.

Ecclesall Woods is one of the largest single areas of ancient woodland in an urban environment in this country. The woods contain a wealth of wild flowers and in springtime is famous for its carpets of bluebells. Broad-leaved trees predominate, including oak, holly, silver birch, beech, larch and Scots pine. Sweet chestnut is a particular speciality although it takes a fine summer to produce nuts big enough for eating. The centre of the woodland is fenced off as a bird sanctuary and in some winters plays hosts to a huge corvid roost attracting thousands of rooks and jackdaws from a wide area – visit at dusk from late autumn into winter to watch the birds pouring in. Cup-and-ring carved stones have been found in Ecclesall Woods, dating from around 2000–1000 BC.

Top and left: Ecclesall Woods

Little is known about these stones – they are possibly maps, or some significant meeting point. The ancient woods were probably cleared for agriculture some 2,000 or more years ago. Ancient fields and some ruins were long ago reclaimed by the ancestors of the trees we see today. More modern sites are the J.G. Graves Woodland Discovery Centre and Abbeydale Miniature Railway.

The trees in Ecclesall Woods were extensively used to produce charcoal from the seventeenth century, fuelling local iron workings, while white coal was made to help in lead smelting. Evidence of these industries is abundant in the woodland, with circular hearths typical of charcoal pits, and keyhole-shaped earthworks representing white coal kilns.

Follow the waymarked route through Ecclesall Woods, often on distinctive cobbled packhorse tracks; continue straight ahead until you reach Abbeydale Road South (A621). We leave Limb Brook now, as it ends its journey as a tributary to the Sheaf.

Whirlow Hall Farm

Just off the route near Whirlow Brook Park, the farm is well worth exploring, either as a stopping point on the walk (there is a footpath to the farm from the sturdy stone bridge in the Limb Valley) or independently. The farm is run by a charitable trust who offer visits to the farm for children who would otherwise not have the opportunity to experience it. They run farm tours for the public at weekends and there is a cafe and farm shop (see website for opening hours).

Whirlow Lane, Sheffield, S11 9QF
0114 262 0986
www.whirlowhallfarm.org

Whinfell Quarry Garden

Stunning gardens in a sheltered quarry setting.
Free admission.

Ecclesall Road South, S11 9QD
www.friendsofwhinfell.org.uk

J.G. Graves Woodland Discovery Centre

Just off the route in Ecclesall Woods, it is well worth visiting to see the contemporary wooden building and to have a well-deserved coffee and cake at the Woodland Coffee Stop (see website for opening hours).

Ecclesall Woods, Abbey Lane, S7 2QZ
0114 235 6348
www.ecclesallwoodscraftcourses.co.uk
www.woodlandcoffee.co.uk

Abbeydale Miniature Railway

A great favourite with local families, children love to ride on the steam and diesel trains on a scenic track in this corner of Ecclesall Woods. There is also a smaller gauge model railway and a small cafe serving hot and cold drinks, cakes and ice cream. Open occasional Sundays in spring and summer; see website for details.

Ecclesall Woods, Abbeydale Road South, S17 3LB
www.sheffieldmodelengineers.com

Below: The Limb Valley, just below Ringinglow Village
Photo: Dom Worrall, Round Sheffield Run

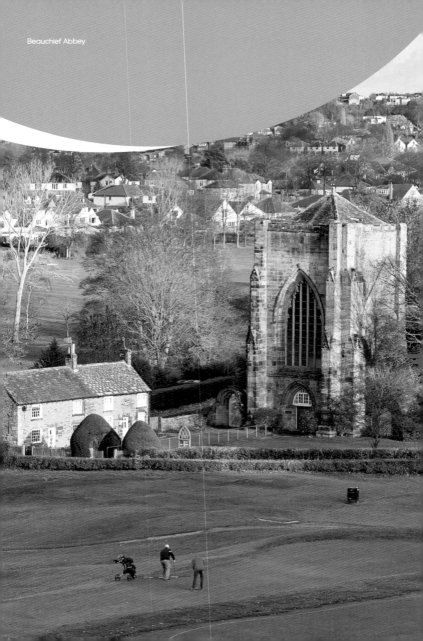
Beauchief Abbey

3
SHEAF VALLEY

Ladies' Spring Wood
Beauchief Abbey
Parkbank Wood
Chancet Wood
Graves Park

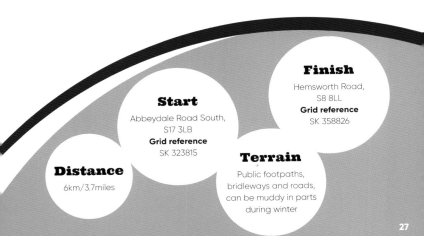

Start

Abbeydale Road South,
S17 3LB
Grid reference
SK 323815

Finish

Hemsworth Road,
S8 8LL
Grid reference
SK 358826

Distance

6km/3.7miles

Terrain

Public footpaths,
bridleways and roads,
can be muddy in parts
during winter

Top left: Woodland in the Sheaf Valley

Top right: Ladies' Spring Wood
Photo: Jon Barton

Right: Ladies' Spring Wood

Turn right along Abbeydale Road South, **cross over** at the first pedestrian lights, and then **turn left** on to Twentywell Lane. The road crosses the River Sheaf (look down and hopefully spy a dipper or grey wagtail) and then the railway; **turn left** on to the footpath into Ladies' Spring Wood. Follow the path up a very steep set of steps. If your timing is spot on the woods will be carpeted in springtime bluebells, taking your mind off the million steps yet to be climbed (there are 106 steps).

Ladies' Spring Wood is an extremely well-preserved example of natural Pennine sessile oak wood (the sessile oak is the tougher sibling to that quintessential English landscape tree the pedunculate oak, and can be differentiated by tall, straight trunks and stalkless acorns) on slopes with acid soils (shales, sandstones and even coal beds) but with a typically alluvial valley bottom giving a much richer vegetation type. It has been designated a site of special scientific interest, and is one of this author's favourite places on the walk. One way the ecologists ascertain whether a wood is ancient or a more recent plantation is the presence of slow-colonising

flowering plants, and Ladies' Spring Wood is full of them, including great wood-rush and common cow-wheat, plus the bluebell, wood sorrel, dog's mercury, yellow archangel, ramsons (wild garlic) and yellow pimpernel.

Keep a bit of an eye on the map and look out for acorn signs through the woods; most paths will lead you to Beauchief Abbey, but crucially not all paths. Once at the top of the hill, **take a left-hand fork** then slightly downhill at the first junction, then at the next split by the interpretation sign **take a right-hand fork** up a few more steps. All too soon you emerge on to Beauchief Drive. **Turn left** and follow the road downhill until you reach Abbey Farm on your right. **Turn right** on to the track between the farm and Beauchief Abbey which leads to Parkbank Wood.

Beauchief Abbey is listed as a scheduled ancient monument. It was founded by Robert FitzRanulph, Lord of Alfreton, Norton and Marnham. Between 1172 and 1176, Beauchief Abbey was dedicated to St Thomas Becket and opened for the reception of an abbot and canons in about 1183.

Top left: Beauchief Abbey Farm

Top right: Parkbank Wood

Right bottom: Beauchief Abbey

The tower of the abbey as it now stands is part of the western tower of the original building. There was a park, including Hutcliffe Wood, attached to the abbey and fish ponds – the fish are still there but they look a bit on the sour side. At first the abbey had five canons and an abbott. In 1537 the abbey was closed down by Henry VIII's commissioner; the abbey and all its properties were surrendered into the hands of Henry VIII.

Parkbank Wood is another of Sheffield's fine oak woods; **follow the path with the golf course to your left**, then uphill. Hard to believe you are in the heart of one of Europe's most industrialised cities.

At the end of Parkbank Wood **cross over** Bocking Lane, **turn right** and after 50 metres **turn left** on to the footpath leading into Chancet Wood. At the footbridge **take the left-hand fork**. This small dell could do with a little more clean water, but the surrounding woodland is once again beautiful. The path winds up and around to the right. The woodland is mixed and was once heavily coppiced. This small strip of woodland is hanging on valiantly with housing developments squeezing it to the right and left, but hanging on it is.

On leaving the wood, **turn right** and use the pedestrian crossing to **cross over** Meadowhead (A61). **Turn left** on to the path into Graves Park. There is a fine finger of woodland running through the centre of the park. We will follow that.

Graves Park is Sheffield's largest park; it was presented to the city between 1925 and 1935 by Alderman J.G. Graves. There are bowling greens, cricket pitches, tennis courts, a miniature golf course, a children's playground, lakes, waterfowl, a bird and sculpture trail, a cafe, animal farm and a popular Saturday morning Parkrun. The animal farm is famed for keeping many rare breeds, and it's only a two-minute diversion from the walk to see the residents.

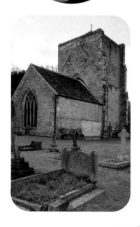

Follow the path through the woods, a sweeping vista of sharp little valleys, rocky outcrops, dog walkers and kids running around like kids do. Pass the rear of the cafe and **leave the park** at the junction of Hemsworth Road and Bunting Nook adjacent to the car park entrance.

Eat, drink and explore

Abbeydale Industrial Hamlet

A short walk off route along Abbeydale Road South, this industrial museum is well worth a visit. Abbeydale Works was once the largest water-powered industrial site on the River Sheaf. See a tilt forge, crucible furnace and a row of restored worker's cottages. Also, there is a learning centre, cafe and shop. Small admission charge; open every day except Fridays.

Abbeydale Road South, S7 2QW
0114 272 2106
www.simt.co.uk

Beauchief Abbey

The abbey is normally only open for services or by prior arrangement with the keyholder. Please contact the abbey direct if you wish to visit. The grounds can be visited when the abbey is closed.

Beauchief Abbey Lane, S8 7BD
www.beauchiefabbey.org.uk

Spoon

Just off the route in Woodseats you'll find this gem of a cafe. From breakfasts and sandwiches to bigger meals and excellent coffee and cake, all food is cooked fresh on the premises, including jam and sauces.

20 Abbey Lane, S8 0BL
0114 274 0014
www.spoon-cafebistro.co.uk

Graves Park Animal Farm

This popular attraction provides a home to some of the rarest breeds of farm animals in the country. You can get up close and personal with Tamworth pigs; Highland cattle and Jacob sheep, plus goats, donkeys, waterfowl, rabbits and many more. Children can also enjoy pretending to drive the farm tractor.
Free admission.

Graves Park, Hemsworth Road, S8 8LJ
0114 250 0500

Rose Garden Cafe

Traditional park cafe serving good, affordable meals, drinks and ice cream. Plenty of indoor and outdoor seating available.

Graves Park, Hemsworth Road, S8 8LJ
0114 258 2705
www.rosegardencafe.co.uk

Below: Beauchief Abbey

Bottom: Woodland in the Sheaf Valley

Meersbrook Park
Photo: Dom Worrall,
Round Sheffield Run

GLEADLESS VALLEY

Gleadless Valley Woodland Park
Coneygree Wood
Bishops' House
Meersbrook Park
Broadfield Park
Sheffield Antiques Quarter
Brincliffe Edge
Chelsea Park
Hunter's Bar Roundabout

Finish
Hunter's Bar Roundabout,
Ecclesall Road, S11 8TF
Grid reference
SK 332857

Start
Hemsworth Road,
S8 8LL
Grid reference
SK 358826

Distance
6.9km/4.3miles

Terrain
Public footpaths,
bridleways and roads,
can be muddy in
parts during winter

Top left and right: Woodland in the Gleadless Valley

Top right: Bluebells

Exit Graves Park and turn right along Hemsworth Road until you see a public house on the opposite side of the road. **Cross the road** here and **turn left** along Ashbury Lane into the tradesmen's entrance to Gleadless Valley Woodland Park which essentially connects nine small ancient woods. As Sheffield expanded, the woods were incorporated along with their original boundaries into the overall design of the huge 1950s housing estates being built. Of course, leaving room for the working classes to have their allotments and the upper classes to have their golf courses. I believe the aspirations of both classes have since switched.

Take the path to the left, adjacent to the hedge and down to a small footbridge. The path passes between Lees Hall Golf Club on your right and Newfield School on your left and descends into Coneygree Wood, an ancient patch of woodland, containing some relic coppicing. **Take the left-hand fork** down to a footbridge then **turn right** to emerge at the end of Lees Hall Avenue.

As you leave the woods Heeley & Meersbrook Allotments are on your right. As with elsewhere on the walk, stretches of woodland adjacent to allotments provide an excellent habitat for both badgers and foxes. Foxes often form dens under the sheds while badgers dig setts in the woods and then raid the allotments by night. To see either your best chance is to be out and about either late or very early. **Walk along** the full length of Lees Hall Avenue, crossing Lees Hall Road on the way, **and turn left** along Upper Albert Road and soon on your right you'll arrive at the entrance to Meersbrook Park at Bishops' House; **turn right** into the park. You will have by now gathered that Sheffield is home to a great community of conservationists; recent initiatives have seen a flourish of wild flower reintroductions. I hope you have been enjoying them so far?

Meersbrook Park was acquired by Sheffield Corporation in 1886, and this park is one of Sheffield's oldest public parks and boasts many features of historical interest. Here you'll find the timber-framed Bishops' House, and

Top: Coneygree Wood

Right: Bishops' House

the former Meersbrook Hall (1780). The latter was once the Ruskin Museum, and later it was used as offices by Sheffield City Council. It is now jointly managed by Heeley Development Trust and the Friends of Meersbrook Hall and used for courses and community events. Much of the landscape of the park is Victorian. There is no mistaking that you are on an urban walk here with its wonderful views over the city.

Walk through the park, leaving at the corner of Meersbrook Park Road and Brook Road. **Walk along** Meersbrook Park Road to Chesterfield Road (A61). Altogether quite urban now, one's stout walking boots, fleece and poles somewhat out of place. **Turn right** along Chesterfield Road, **cross over** using the pedestrian crossing, **turn left** back along Chesterfield Road then **turn right** on to Little London Road. **Pass under** the railway bridge, follow the road round to the left, then immediately **turn right** on to the footpath and cycle track link through the business park to meet up with the River Sheaf again. After the footbridge **veer left**

Top left: Meersbrook Park
Photo: Dom Worrall,
Round Sheffield Run

Top right: Views from
Meersbrook Park

Right: Bishops' House

and **cross over** Broadfield Way to follow the short route by the river through our smallest park, Broadfield Park. Say goodbye to the Sheaf; say hello to the Sheffield Antiques Quarter. You will have seen the ubiquitous grey squirrel nearly everywhere on the walk, while rabbits, foxes, badgers and other small mammals may also have been seen. Keep an eye out for bats, common in most of the parks. But before you leave the Sheaf, pause and look once more at the water; in time, one of us will spy a feeding otter, perhaps on this bit of the Sheaf, or in one of the millponds. Keep glancing across the water because one day it will happen.

Leave the park on to Leyburn Road; walk along the road, then **turn left** along and cross Abbeydale Road, using the pedestrian crossing. Now, with the school on your right, **turn right** along Glen Road, then **turn left** along Sandford Grove Road until you reach Brincliffe Edge. Unlike many woods in urban Sheffield, this woodland is a nineteenth-century plantation. The wood is mainly oak and beech. Beautiful trees and charming stone-built Victorian houses hang on to this ridge of land.

Follow the path along the top of the woodland. The path then descends into the woods and back up to Brincliffe Edge Road. **Cross over** the road and enter Chelsea Park, which is an attractive small park in Nether Edge. It once formed the grounds of Brincliffe Towers, which was owned by Robert Styring, a former Lord Mayor of Sheffield. Sunny spring days in Chelsea Park bring out a variety of butterflies which include the speckled wood, tortoiseshell, peacock, meadow brown and rarer comma. Keep an ear open, too, for the noisy tropical squawk of the rose-ringed parakeet, an escaped species slowly building up a feral population in this area.

Follow the main path through Chelsea Park. As you leave the park, **turn left** along Chelsea Road and take the **first right** into Cavendish Road. At the end of the road **turn left** along Osborne Road and **cross over** Psalter Lane. Walk down Stretton Road. And if you keep heading downhill, following the signs, you'll end up back at Hunter's Bar Roundabout.

Eat, drink and explore

Bishops' House

Visit the best surviving sixteenth-century timber-framed house in Sheffield. Used as accommodation for employees of Sheffield City Council until 1974, it became a museum in 1976. The house is managed by the Friends of Bishops' House, a voluntary organisation, who run events and activities in the house. Open at weekends; free admission.

Lees Hall Avenue, S8 9NA
0114 255 7701
www.bishopshouse.org.uk

Just Falafs

A hidden gem near Meersbrook Park, this vegan cafe makes a delicious lunch stop. Enjoy homemade falafel with hummus and pitta, and help yourself to a selection of salads. See website for opening hours.

87 Chesterfield Road, S8 0RN
0114 255 0697
www.just-falafs.co.uk

The Broadfield

Best known for serving an ever-changing array of pies. The Broadfield also stocks a wide selection of real ales and has over a hundred types of whiskey to choose from.

452 Abbeydale Road, S7 1FR
0114 255 0200
www.thebroadfield.co.uk

Porter Pizza Company

Just off Hunter's Bar Roundabout on the ever-popular Sharrow Vale Road you'll find top-class, authentic wood-fired pizzas. There are a few stools to eat inside or take your pizza into Endcliffe Park. Open every day.

410 Sharrow Vale Road, S11 8ZP
0114 267 6672
www.porterpizza.co.uk

The Street Food Chef: Mexican Canteen

A little bit further along Sharrow Vale Road you'll come to this family run eatery, promising healthy fast food. Choose from burritos, tacos and quesadillas; gluten-free and dairy-free options are available. Open every day.

376 Sharrow Vale Road, S11 2ZP
0114 327 4778
www.streetfoodchef.co.uk

Seven Hills Bakery and Cafe

A short walk further along Sharrow Vale Road, opposite the junction with Ashford Road, you'll find this popular, informal cafe. Serving a simple menu that showcases local fresh produce; the bread and savouries are baked on the premises. Open 9.00 a.m. until 3.00 p.m. daily.

232 Sharrow Vale Road, S11 8ZP
0114 267 0133
www.sevenhillsbakery.co.uk

Shortcuts

The walk can be shortened by using local buses to either return to the start point or just to miss a section out if you want to. Frequent buses run along Ecclesall Road South and Ecclesall Road (use this to get from part-way through the Limb Valley section back to the start at Hunter's Bar Roundabout) and along Abbeydale Road South and Abbeydale Road (use this to get from the start of the Sheaf Valley section to part way through the Gleadless Valley section). See transport information opposite.

More Walks

The Blue Loop

The Blue Loop is a continuous loop of the waterways and riverside walkways in the heart of Sheffield, made up of the River Don, Five Weirs Walk and the Sheffield and Tinsley Canal. This circular eight-mile walk follows the Sheffield and Tinsley Canal from its terminus at Victoria Quays canal basin out to the east, following the locks of Tinsley flight to where the canal joins the River Don at Meadowhall.

It then follows the Five Weirs Walk along the River Don back to the city centre. The walk is varied and interesting, very industrial, sometimes picturesque, and not short of an incredible and often surprising amount of wildlife. The Friends of the Blue Loop is a volunteer-led organisation that maintains and improves this area of Sheffield; a detailed route map and information about shorter walks in the area are available at www.the-rsc.co.uk/riverlution/friends-of-the-blue-loop

Upper Don Walk

The Upper Don Walk is a six-mile-long linear walk which links the centre of Sheffield to the village of Oughtibridge. The route makes the best of the congested urban landscape but at times the river is conspicuous by its absence.

Trans Pennine Trail

The Trans Pennine Trail is a coast-to-coast trail linking the west coast at Southport to the east coast at Hornsea near Hull. It is designed for walkers, cyclists and horse riders and takes in some of the best scenery in Northern England. The trail now has a spur running through Sheffield and on to Chesterfield where it traverses the River Don, the Sheffield and Tinsley Canal and the River Rother. Extensive information is available at www.transpenninetrail.org.uk.

Tourist Information

www.theoutdoorcity.co.uk
www.welcometosheffield.co.uk
www.ourfaveplaces.co.uk

Transport Information

The starting point of the walk as well as many places along the route are accessible by public transport. This website includes a useful travel planner:
www.travelsouthyorkshire.com
01709 515151.

Outdoor Shops

Foothills

Based near the route in Nether Edge, Foothills is an independent outdoor equipment specialist for hill and mountain walkers, travellers and their families.
11 Edgedale Road, S7 2BQ
0114 258 6228
www.foothills.co.uk

myRaceKit

An independent specialist running shop based very near the route at Hunter's Bar.
296–298 Sharrow Vale Road, S11 8ZL
0114 266 9591
www.frontrunnersheffield.co.uk

Accelerate

Large independent running shop based in Attercliffe.
629 Attercliffe Road, S9 3RD
0114 242 2569
www.accelerateuk.com

Weather

www.metoffice.gov.uk

Hotels

The Florentine

Tapton Park Road, S10 3FG
0114 230 8692
www.theflorentinepub.com

The Norfolk Arms

2 Ringinglow Village, S11 7TS
0114 230 2197
www.norfolkarms.com

Halifax Hall Boutique Hotel

Endcliffe Vale Road, S10 3ER
0114 222 8810
www.halifaxhall.co.uk

Brocco on the Park

92 Brocco Bank, S11 8RS
0114 266 1233
www.brocco.co.uk

Copthorne Hotel

Bramall Lane, S2 4SU
0114 252 5480
www.millenniumhotels.com/en/sheffield/copthorne-hotel-sheffield

The Outdoor City

About the Author

Jon Barton is the founder of Vertebrate Publishing, Britain's number one publisher of outdoor activity and adventure books. He's the author of Vertebrate's best-selling *Peak District Mountain Biking* and *White Peak Mountain Biking* guides, as well as climbing and trail running guidebooks to the Peak District. A keen runner, climber, mountain biker and fell walker, Jon has a huge amount of experience travelling the world in search of adventures, but loves coming home to Sheffield where his favourite adventures always start.

Vertebrate Publishing

At Vertebrate Publishing we publish books to inspire adventure.

It's our rule that the only books we publish are those that we'd want to read or use ourselves. We endeavour to bring you beautiful books that stand the test of time and that you'll be proud to have on your bookshelf for years to come.

The Peak District was the inspiration behind our first books. Our offices are situated on its doorstep, minutes away from world-class climbing, biking and hillwalking. We're driven by our own passion for the outdoors, for exploration, and for the natural world; it's this passion that we want to share with our readers.

We aim to inspire everyone to get out there. We want to connect readers – young and old – with the outdoors and the positive impact it can have on well-being. We think it's particularly important that young people get outside and explore the natural world, something we support through our publishing programme.

As well as publishing award-winning new books, we're working to make available many out-of-print classics in both print and digital formats. These are stories that we believe are unique and significant; we want to make sure that they continue to be shared and enjoyed.

www.v-publishing.co.uk